0508005

W9-BXO-990

'LINE

JBIOG
Gersh
Whiting, Jim

**The Life and Times of George
Gershwin**

Masters of Music
THE WORLD'S GREATEST COMPOSERS

The Life and Times of

George Gershwin

Mitchell Lane
PUBLISHERS

P.O. Box 196
Hockessin, Delaware 19707

Masters of Music

THE WORLD'S GREATEST COMPOSERS

Titles in the Series

The Life and Times of...

Visit us on the web: www.mitchelllane.com
Comments? email us: mitchelllane@mitchelllane.com

Masters of Music
THE WORLD'S GREATEST COMPOSERS

The Life and Times of
George Gershwin

by Jim Whiting

Printing   1   2   3   4   5   6   7   8
        Library of Congress Cataloging-in-Publication Data
Whiting, Jim, 1943-
        The life and times of George Gershwin/Jim Whiting.
            p. cm. — (Masters of music)
        Includes bibliographical references (p.) and index.
            ISBN 1-58415-279-6 (library bound)
        1. Gershwin, George, 1989-1937—Juvenile literature. 2. Composers—United States—Biography—Juvenile literature. I. Title. II. Series.
        ML3930.G29W55 2004
        780'.92—dc22
                                                                        2004009312

ABOUT THE AUTHOR: Jim Whiting has been a journalist, writer, editor, and photographer for more than 20 years. In addition to a lengthy stint as publisher of *Northwest Runner* magazine, Mr. Whiting has contributed articles to the *Seattle Times*, *Conde Nast Traveler*, *Newsday*, and *Saturday Evening Post*. He has written and edited more than 100 Mitchell Lane titles. His great love of music inspired him to write this book. He lives in Washington state with his wife and two teenage sons.

PHOTO CREDITS: Cover, pp. 1, 3, 5, 6 Getty Images; p. 13 North Wind Photos; pp. 19, 25, 31, 37 Getty Images

PUBLISHER'S NOTE: This story is based on the author's extensive research, which he believes to be accurate. Documentation of such research is contained on page 46.

The internet sites referenced herein were active as of the publication date. Due to the fleeting nature of some web sites, we cannot guarantee they will all be active when you are reading this book.

Contents

The Life and Times of

George Gershwin

by Jim Whiting

  * For Your Information

The official mascot of the 1984 Olympic Games, Sam the Eagle, marches around the Los Angeles Coliseum during the opening ceremonies. With the Olympics virtually in the shadow of Hollywood, it seemed appropriate that the Walt Disney Company designed Sam.

National Pride

As thousands of spectators filed into the Los Angeles Coliseum on July 28, 1984, for the opening ceremonies of the Olympic Games, there was an excited buzz of anticipation. It was the first time that the Summer Olympics had been held on American soil since 1932. The organizers were determined that what was about to be seen by nearly 100,000 people inside the Coliseum and by 2.5 billion more on live television around the world would not only showcase the athletes but also the American way of life.

The Games came at a good time in American history. Following the heavy American involvement in the Vietnam War that began in 1964, the country had been deeply divided. Nearly 60,000 American servicemen and servicewomen were killed before the final withdrawal in 1975. It was the first time that the country had lost a war. The final stages were especially humiliating. A long line of people, waiting to be evacuated, stretched from the roof of the American embassy down through the building. A continual stream of helicopters flew in, snatched up a few people at a time, and flew them to the safety of an aircraft carrier lying offshore. The airlift was the only way out. The communists controlled all the land exits. These images of American helplessness were transmitted all over the world.

With bitterness from the war still lingering, a further shock awaited the country in November 1979. A mob of Iranians poured into the American Embassy in Tehran, Iran's capital. Fifty-two Americans were seized as hostages. The United States protested, but to no avail. The following month, troops from the Soviet Union invaded Afghanistan. Again the United States protested. Again it did no good. In 1980, eight American soldiers died when a mission to rescue the hostages in Iran ended in a well-publicized failure. To many people, these were more signs that the U.S. was continuing to lose its military power.

Then perceptions began to change. The American hostages were finally released early in 1981. While their freedom came as the result of diplomacy rather than military action, people were relieved that these Americans were no longer in captivity. In 1982, a popular film called *First Blood* appeared on movie screens. It features actor Sylvester Stallone as Vietnam veteran John Rambo. Several previous films had depicted Vietnam veterans as embittered, helpless men. Some were dependent on drugs. Rambo is just the opposite. He is a strong, highly trained soldier who refuses to back down from anyone. When local police officials arrest him just for passing through town, he fights for what he believes in. American audiences appreciated this new perspective on Vietnam vets and looked at Rambo as a hero.

In 1979, a communist government backed by Cuban dictator Fidel Castro had taken control of the Caribbean island nation of Grenada. A military coup in 1983 resulted in more than 100 deaths. The U.S. government, already concerned about Castro's increasing influence in the Caribbean, now feared for the safety of a number of American students in Grenada. President Ronald Reagan ordered an invasion by U.S. troops, who quickly secured a victory. Even though it was an uneven fight, many Americans were elated about the win. After the depressing years when the Vietnam War had dragged on and on, any win was welcome and helped restore American pride in its military.

As a result of these and other developments, the mood of the country was becoming more optimistic by the time the Olympics approached. Americans were proud of their country again. The Los Angeles Olympic

Games would be the ideal way of showing this pride. There was another reason for emphasizing the American way of life. At that time, the United States and the Soviet Union had been locked in a cold war for several decades. Even though the two nations had been allies in their effort to defeat Nazi Germany in World War II, their systems of government were entirely different. Both sides maintained staggering arsenals, including enough nuclear weapons to virtually wipe out the other's population.

These political differences carried over into the Olympics. In 1980, the Games had been held in Moscow, the capital of the Soviet Union. It was the first time that a communist country had hosted the Olympics. Like the Americans, the Soviets wanted the Olympics to serve as a showcase for the advantages of their way of life. They were therefore shocked and disappointed when U.S. President Jimmy Carter refused to allow American athletes to compete in the Olympics. He was protesting the Soviet invasion of Afghanistan. He also urged other countries to boycott the Games. As a result, more than sixty nations stayed away from Moscow.

It wasn't surprising that the Soviets retaliated by boycotting the 1984 Games. Sixteen nations joined them. However, this boycott would not affect the profitability of the Games. Because the 1976 Olympics in Montreal had lost huge sums of money, the organizers of the 1984 Games allowed more than forty companies to purchase the rights to sell "official" Olympic merchandise to cover the costs of producing the Games. The 1984 Games would make a profit of $150 million.

The opening ceremonies were organized by David L. Wolper, a movie and television producer whose credits included the 1977 television epic *Roots*. *Roots* had been the first blockbuster miniseries. It appeared on eight successive nights and was about a young African man who had been sold into slavery; it followed his story through several generations of his descendents. The miniseries drew huge audiences and won nine Emmy awards.

Wolper organized many spectacular special effects for the three-and-a-half-hour extravaganza. Church bells rang out all over the Los Angeles area. An airplane flew overhead, spelling *WELCOME* in huge letters. A man wearing a rocket pack flew into the Coliseum and landed in the middle of the field. Thousands of pigeons fluttered up into the air. A huge marching band paraded up and down as its more than 800 members played popular songs. Covered wagons raced across the infield. Even the audience became involved. They were given large colored cards and special instructions so that they could display the national flags of the participating nations.

For many people, the most sensational part came when eighty-four pianists played eighty-four grand pianos. Just getting the pianos ready to go was a major achievement. They had to be trucked into the Coliseum and installed, then each one had to be carefully and painstakingly tuned. They also had to be protected from the sunshine. When all was ready, the pianists—wearing matching blue tuxedos—played *Rhapsody in Blue.*

In many ways, it was an excellent choice of music. Its composer had been born to immigrant parents who had arrived in the United States near the end of the nineteenth century with almost no money. Their son was a high school dropout who began working full-time when he was fifteen. Within a decade, *Rhapsody in Blue* and other works he had composed made him famous around the world. He seemed to be the perfect embodiment of the American Dream—someone who became successful and famous entirely through his own efforts.

His name is George Gershwin.◆

Sports and Politics

Adolf Hitler

The 1980 and 1984 Olympics weren't the first ones to involve politics. In 1976, many African nations wanted to keep New Zealand out of the Olympics because the country's rugby team had toured South Africa. At that time, South Africa's government was enforcing apartheid, a policy of rigid racial separation. New Zealand's rugby tour broke an international agreement not to play South African teams as a way to protest apartheid. By breaking the agreement, New Zealand was seen as supporting the segregation. When New Zealand was allowed to participate in the Olympics, more than twenty African nations stayed away.

Perhaps the most famous instance came in 1936. German dictator Adolf Hitler tried to use the Berlin Olympics in the same way that Americans would in 1984: to demonstrate the superiority of the people and the way of life in his country. For many, though, Germany's way of life was frightening. Hitler had already demonstrated his extreme prejudice against Jews. Some people urged the United States to boycott the Berlin Games in protest, but the U.S. Olympic Committee voted to participate. Though Germany won more medals than any other country, African-American athlete Jesse Owens won four gold medals—his wins were seen as undermining Hitler's belief in German superiority.

Politics have also influenced the results of individual competitions. During the Mexico City Olympics in 1968, American athletes John Carlos and Tommie Smith won the gold and bronze medals in the 200 meters. During the playing of "The Star-Spangled Banner" at the awards ceremony, both men looked downward while raising black-gloved fists in the "Black Power" salute. They were demonstrating against racial injustice in their own country. Because they tried to use their win to promote their political beliefs, they were kicked off the team and sent home.

Twelve years earlier, the Olympics were held soon after the Soviet Union had crushed an uprising in Hungary. Teams representing the two nations met in a water polo match. The Hungarians won 4-0. The athletes hit, bit, and scratched each other, and the contest became known as the "Blood in the Water" match. The climax of the violence came when a Soviet player sucker-punched Ervin Zador, the Hungarian star. A photo of Zador with blood steaming down his face was shown all over the world as a symbol of Soviet tyranny.

Immigrants to the United States during the end of the nineteenth century wait to be processed at Ellis Island in New York City harbor. George Gershwin's parents came to the United States from Russia and passed through Ellis Island.

Masters of Music

CHAPTER 2

From the Streets to the Piano

Sometime during the early 1890s, a young Russian named Moishe Gershovitz had to make a difficult decision. The girl he loved, Rose Bruskin, had moved with her family to the United States. Moishe wanted to be with her, but that would mean leaving his native land behind.

In reality, there wasn't much to keep him in Russia. He had a menial job with a very limited future. There was a good chance he'd be drafted into the Russian army—for a period of up to twenty-five years. Even worse, Moishe was Jewish. There was a great deal of prejudice against Jews, called anti-Semitism, in Russia. Jews were often the victims of pogroms, organized riots that injured or killed many Jewish people and destroyed their property.

It's not surprising that Moishe decided to follow Rose. As often happened during that era, his name was changed as soon as he entered the United States. He became known as Morris Gershvin. In 1895, he and Rose were married. They set up a home in New York City and began a family. Their first child, a son named Ira, was born in 1896.

Their second son, George, was born on September 26, 1898. The name on his birth certificate actually reads "Jacob Gershwine." The boy was named for his grandfather, but no one ever called him anything besides George. The doctor who recorded his birth misspelled the last name.

Morris and Rose would have two more children: Arthur was born in 1900 and the one girl, Francis (more commonly known by her nickname of Frankie), was born in 1906.

By the time of Frankie's birth, George had acquired a reputation in the neighborhood. It wasn't a good one. Many years later, Frankie would recall, "George was a pretty wild boy. People used to say, 'Mrs. Gershwin has nice children, but that son of hers, she's going to have trouble with that son, George.'"[1]

George was a tough kid who enjoyed being on the streets, where he played games such as stickball, street hockey, and handball. He also became an excellent roller skater. His skating came in handy on at least one occasion. A gang of Irish boys chased him, but he managed to speed away on his skates. In his eagerness to escape, he didn't notice that he was entering a construction site. He tripped and fell down an elevator shaft, giving himself a concussion.

That wasn't his only injury. Because he was so competitive, he often got into fights. His nose was broken probably more than once.

One reason for George's wildness might have been that the Gershvins were not a typical immigrant family, with a working father and stay-at-home mother. Morris was a restless man who worked at a variety of jobs and started several businesses of his own. These included a bakery, a Turkish bath, several restaurants, a cigar store, a pool hall, and even a stint as a bookmaker. Rose kept a careful eye on him, often working beside him. That frequently left the children with little or no parental supervision. The family also moved a great deal, living in twenty-eight different apartments between 1898 and 1916.

These conditions didn't seem to affect Ira, the oldest child. He was quiet, obedient, and did well in school. By the time he was fourteen, he would be admitted to a school for exceptional students. George couldn't have been more different.

As Ira remembered, "We never had much in common as kids. I was always home reading. George would always be out on the street, playing with the boys and girls. He would get into street fights and come home with black eyes, etc. He had his own life, and I had mine. We were in two completely different worlds."[2]

These differences were reflections of their parents. Morris was an easygoing man who didn't let many things bother him. Rose was more serious. She made demands on George. Because both Rose and George were strong-willed, they often clashed. It didn't help that George repeatedly got into trouble at school.

Despite George's dislike for school, his interest in music began there. It came about by pure chance. Up to the time he was ten, he thought that music was only appropriate for girls. Then one of his younger classmates, a future famous violinist named Max Rosen, gave a concert at an assembly. George decided that he would rather be outside on the playground with his buddies than listening to "sissy stuff."

He couldn't escape the sound of Max's playing as it came out through an open window. As the early eighteenth-century writer William Congreve wrote in his play *The Mourning Bride,* "Music has charms to soothe a savage breast." The music definitely worked its charms on the savage George, for he suddenly stopped playing and began listening intently. When the last notes died away, George decided that he wanted to meet the young violinist. There was only one problem: He couldn't go back inside. If he did, his absence would surely be noticed. So he waited outside in a heavy rain. By the time he snuck back into the building, he was too late. Max had gone home.

George was persistent. As he wrote later, "I found out where he lived and, dripping wet as I was, trekked to his house, unceremoniously presenting myself as an admirer. Maxie, by this time, had left. His family were so amused, however, that they arranged a meeting. From the first moment we became the closest of friends."[3]

Their friendship, however, proved to be short-lived. George wanted to become Max's accompanist. Max wasn't interested. And he wasn't content to just say no.

George remembered, "There came a climactic day when he told me flatly that I had better give up all thought of a musical career. 'You haven't got it in you, Georgie; take my word for it, I can tell.'"[4]

Fortunately, George had enough self-confidence not to be discouraged. By that time he had discovered another outlet for his musical ambitions. His mother decided to buy a secondhand upright piano. She intended it for Ira, who wasn't all that excited about playing the piano. Then a strange thing happened.

"The upright had scarcely been put in place when George twirled the stool down to size, sat, lifted the keyboard cover, and played an accomplished version of a then popular song," Ira recalled. "I remember being particularly impressed by his swinging, lightning fast left hand, and by harmonic and rhythmic effects I thought as proficient as those of most of the pianists I'd heard in vaudeville. . . . How? When? We wanted to know. George made it sound it very simple. Whenever he had the chance, he'd been fooling around and experimenting on a player piano at the home of a schoolmate around the corner on Seventh. So, with little discussion, it was decided that the lesson-taker would be George."[5]

George was transformed.

"Studying the piano made a good boy out of a bad one," he recalled years later. "It took the piano to tone me down. It made me more serious. I was a changed person six months after I took it up."[6]

The change didn't meet with complete approval at home. His father, who enjoyed music, was proud to see that his son was playing at school assemblies. His mother was more practical. Because her husband's income was often inconsistent, she wanted to make sure that George studied something that would provide a secure financial future. For her, that "something" was accounting. At her urging, George entered the High School of Commerce when he was fourteen.

George would soon become very interested in commerce. But it wasn't the accounting that his mother had in mind. ◆

The Spanish-American War

USS Maine

Starting with Columbus's voyage to the New World in 1492, the Spanish quickly built up the world's largest colonial empire. Four hundred years later, it was reduced to a handful of possessions, most notably Cuba and the Philippine Islands. Even there, local people were trying to overthrow their Spanish masters.

The United States was especially interested in Cuba because American companies had invested a lot of money to help grow Cuban sugar. Many Americans also resented the harsh control that Spanish authorities exercised over the Cuban people. The strained relations came to a head when the battleship USS *Maine* blew up while anchored in the harbor of Havana, the Cuban capital, on February 15, 1898. More than 250 sailors died. Several U.S. newspapers blamed Spain, even though no one knows even today what caused the explosion. The public demanded action. They got it on April 25, 1898, when Congress declared war.

The conflict that followed was very one-sided. American warships destroyed a Spanish fleet in Manila Bay in the Philippines on May 1. American troops landed in Cuba in June. On July 1, Theodore Roosevelt became a national hero when he led a charge up San Juan Hill near Santiago, Cuba's second-largest city. Two days later, American naval forces won another overwhelming victory, destroying a Spanish fleet based in Santiago. Several months afterward, the two sides signed a peace treaty. The United States took over the islands of Guam and Puerto Rico and purchased the Philippines from Spain. Cuba was granted its independence, though the United States retained ownership of Guantánamo Bay, a superb natural harbor in the southeastern corner of the island.

About 3,000 Americans died in the conflict, though about 90 percent of these deaths were caused by disease rather than combat. The war marked the emergence of the United States as a major power on the international stage.

George Gershwin (on the left) and fellow songwriter Irving Berlin pose at the edge of a New York City pier, both wearing clothing that reflect the style of the times.

CHAPTER

3

Tin Pan Alley

After briefly studying with two teachers, George Gershwin met Charles Hambitzer, a versatile musician who composed and played the piano and viola in addition to giving lessons. It was a sort of musical match made in heaven.

"I have a new pupil who will make his mark in music if anybody will," Hambitzer wrote soon after giving George his first lessons. "The boy is a genius, without a doubt; he's just crazy about music and can't wait until it's time to take his lesson."[1]

George was just as excited. He learned the music of such masters as Wolfgang Amadeus Mozart and Frédéric Chopin, as well as contemporary music, including the songs of Irving Berlin. Berlin was just ten years older than George but was already famous all over the country.

George realized that he wanted to devote his life to music. Early in 1914, he heard about a job opening with Jerome H. Remick and Company, a music publishing company on Tin Pan Alley. Tin Pan Alley was a single block of West Twenty-Eighth Street, between Fifth and Sixth Avenues, in Manhattan. Many music publishers were concentrated there. It got its name one hot summer when a man named Monroe Rosenfeld compared the sound coming from many pianos being played with the windows open to the clanging and banging of dozens of pots and pans.

In the early days of the twentieth century, just as in the early days of the twenty-first, there was a lot of money to be made in the music industry. At that time, however, hardly anyone owned record players or radios. Movies with sound were more than a decade away. Television lay even further in the future. But many people owned pianos or knew someone who did. So the primary way of making money in music was publishing sheet music that people could play on their pianos. Music companies were continually coming up with new songs. A big hit could sell thousands of copies. To introduce their songs to the public, the companies hired "song pluggers." These pianists were jammed into tiny cubicles just large enough to hold a piano and a customer or two. They would play the company's new songs over and over, hoping that customers would buy them. When their workday was over, many of them headed for bars and nightclubs to give the new songs even more exposure.

At fifteen, George had a lot of self-confidence. He walked into Remick's office in March 1914, performed an audition, and was hired as a song plugger for a salary of fifteen dollars a week. He convinced his doubting mother to let him drop out of school.

Even though he was the youngest song plugger in Tin Pan Alley, George soon acquired a reputation as Remick's best musician. He also acquired some new friends. Fred and Adele Astaire, a brother-and-sister dance team about the same age as George, were frequent visitors. The three ambitious teenagers shared their dreams for the future. George said, "Wouldn't it be great if I could write a musical show and you could be in it?"[2]

Playing the same songs over and over again eventually became boring. It wasn't long before George began improvising, or making up new melodies. He showed the ones he thought were the best to his employer. Remick wasn't interested. He had hired the young man to plug songs, not write them.

George wasn't easily discouraged. He simply started knocking on other doors in Tin Pan Alley. Early in 1916, another publisher bought one of his songs. It was entitled "When You Want 'Em, You Can't Get 'Em, When You Got 'Em, You Don't Want 'Em." He hoped the song would earn him a lot of money, since songs were paid on a royalty basis. While he was wrong about that—he only made five dollars from the song—it did have one major impact on his life. He spelled his last name as "Gershwin" on the cover. Soon everyone else in the family adopted the same spelling.

A new occupation followed the new name. George was becoming even more bored with song plugging. The next step up his career ladder was getting a job on Broadway. Broadway is a street in the heart of New York with many theaters. In the early 1900s, audiences flocked there for musical comedies and revues, which were series of short acts that usually included songs. After three years with Remick, George quit and found a job as a rehearsal pianist for a revue called *Miss 1917*. The show was a flop, but George's time there was a success. He not only became popular with the singers, but he also used the opportunity to play some of the songs he had written. Soon his songs were being performed in musicals, even though he didn't get credit for them.

His reputation began to spread. A music publisher named Max Dreyfus hired George to write songs for him at a salary of thirty-five dollars a week. In 1919, Alex Aarons, a producer, chose George to write the entire score for a new musical called *La, La, Lucille*. Once again the production didn't do well. But George was about to hit the big time.

Since the end of World War I the previous November, attendance at Broadway productions had been increasing. People were ready to have a good time. There was an even better market for new songs. George and Irving Caesar, his lyricist, sat down at dinner and sketched a song they thought could become a hit, then went to the Gershwin apartment and finished it that same evening. They took the first word of nineteenth-century composer Stephen Foster's immortal "Swanee River" as their title. To their disappointment, few people bought "Swanee," even though it was given a lavish staging.

Then show-business lightning struck. George went to a party that Broadway star Al Jolson was also attending. Jolson (who would later achieve immortality with his appearance in *The Jazz Singer,* the first motion picture with sound) called himself "America's Greatest Entertainer." He listened as George picked out the melody of "Swanee" on the piano. Impressed, he included it in his current show. It was a sensation. Within the next year, eager buyers snapped up more than two million copies of the sheet music. George and Caesar each made $10,000 in royalties that year for what was little more than a night's work in creating the song. It was destined to become the most popular song that George ever wrote.

Just as important, George was finally in the big-time. He was a player.

Another Famous Songwriter

Irving Berlin

After the terrorist attacks on American soil on September 11, 2001, the most popular song in the United States was "God Bless America." It was composed by Irving Berlin, whose life was similar to George Gershwin's in many ways. Berlin's origins were also in Russia—he was born there in 1888 as Israel Baline. His family came to the United States a few years later. Making money was a constant struggle. Israel left home when he was thirteen and began singing in taverns to support himself. He published his first song, "Marie from Sunny Italy," when he was nineteen. The title page listed his name as "I. Berlin." He decided that he liked his "new" last name better and changed "Israel" to "Irving" because it sounded more "American."

Soon he began working in Tin Pan Alley as a songwriter. In 1911 he published "Alexander's Ragtime Band." It became very successful, selling hundreds of thousands of copies and making him a rich man. Within a few years he had written so many popular songs that he became known as the Hit-Maker.

He wrote a number of Broadway musicals and established his own music publishing company. Then he wrote several film scores. In 1934, he was so famous that he appeared on the cover of *Time* magazine. In 1938, he wrote "God Bless America" on the twentieth anniversary of the end of World War I. Two years later, he wrote "White Christmas." For many years, "White Christmas" was the best-selling record of any type.

Berlin had thirty-five number-one hits during the course of his long career, more than any other composer in history. But his popularity faded with the rise of rock and roll in the late 1950s. He became more and more of a recluse as he got older, rarely appearing in public. He died in 1989 at the age of 101.

George Gershwin sits at a piano in a New York City studio, making the final changes to one of the hundreds of musical compositions that he wrote during his short but very productive career.

CHAPTER 4

Rhapsody in Blue

George began a five-year association with dancer George White when he wrote the music for White's revue *Scandals of 1920*. Two years later, the *Scandals of 1922* became notable for two reasons. One was "I'll Build a Stairway to Paradise." Staged with two huge spiral staircases and fifty dancers, it was one of George's most memorable songs. The other was a miniature opera called "Blue Monday." It was set in an African-American neighborhood in New York; because many theaters would not hire African-American performers, it featured white singers and dancers in blackface. It had a sad ending, which disappointed audiences who were expecting comedy. But one man was impressed. He was Paul Whiteman, a famous bandleader. Whiteman liked the way that George mixed the rhythms of jazz with a more traditional classical style.

Early in 1923, George crossed the Atlantic Ocean for the first time. He composed the music for *Rainbow,* a new musical that was opening in London. When he got off the ship in the port of Southampton, the customs officer asked, "George Gershwin, the composer of 'Swanee'?"[1] George was pleased at this evidence of his growing fame. He wasn't as pleased by the reception given to his music. He later admitted that *Rainbow* was one of his weakest scores, and it didn't do very well.

When George returned to the United States, Whiteman approached him with an idea. He wanted to make jazz more popular among traditional concertgoers and asked George to write a new piece that combined piano and orchestra. It would be part of a concert he was planning called "An Experiment in Modern Music." George made a few sketches, but he was so busy with his Broadway work that he didn't spend a lot of time on the idea. He wasn't even sure that Whiteman was serious about putting on his concert.

On the evening of January 3, 1924, George was playing billiards while his brother Ira was reading the newspaper. Ira saw a small article about the concert that Whiteman had planned. To his astonishment, he read, "George Gershwin is at work on a jazz concerto."[2]

George wasn't quite as surprised because of his previous conversation with Whiteman. But the timing shocked him. The concert would be given on Lincoln's birthday, February 12. That was just over five weeks away. He called Whiteman and tried to explain that he couldn't write a piece that quickly. The bandleader was persuasive, however, and George set to work a few days later. He would write a composition for piano and orchestra, though there was one change from what was printed in the newspaper. The new work wouldn't be a concerto, which had to conform to certain rules of composition. George decided to write a rhapsody, a more free-form piece.

Ira came up with the title. He had recently visited an art gallery that exhibited the works of painter James McNeill Whistler. Whistler had used colors as part of his titles. For example, what is popularly known as *Whistler's Mother*—one of the most famous paintings by an American—is formally known as *Arrangement in Gray and Black*. In addition to jazz, Ira knew that his brother was going to include elements of the blues in his new composition. Why not *Rhapsody in Blue*? he suggested.

That did it. George was off and running—literally. A few days later he was on a train to Boston when he had an "Aha!" moment. As he described it later, "It was on the train, with its steely rhythms, its rattle-ty bang that is often so stimulating to a composer. . . . And there I suddenly heard—

and even saw on paper—the complete construction of the rhapsody, from beginning to end. I heard it as a sort of musical kaleidoscope of America—of our vast melting pot, of our unduplicated national pep, of our blues, our metropolitan madness. By the time I reached Boston I had a definite plot of the piece."[3]

George completed the work in three weeks. It would make him immortal.

Rhapsody in Blue was the next-to-last composition on the program. Up to that point, the concert had been a failure. The audience was bored with the selections that Whiteman had made. Many people were about ready to walk out. Their attitude changed as soon as the clarinet seemed to wail *Rhapsody*'s opening bars. Then George's fingers flew across the keyboard. The audience sat, almost breathless, as they listened to the new work. They were carried along with its energy and vitality, its jazzy rhythms and catchy tunes. When the final notes died away sixteen minutes later, there was a momentary hush.

"A crescendo of tumultuous applause and enthusiastic cries swept the house," writes Charles Schwartz. "Members of the audience were standing and clapping and cheering wildly in their enthusiasm for the composer and his piece. Gershwin was recalled again and again in response to the vociferous outcries of pleasure that greeted him and his work."[4]

The audience included many of New York's leading drama critics. While many of them found some faults with the new piece, their overall impressions were favorable. One said, "This young man of twenty-five had written the finest piece of serious music that had ever come out of America."[5]

Later that year Gershwin went back to England. This time his musical, *Primrose,* was a success. When he returned, he began working on a new Broadway musical, *Lady, Be Good!* He had a new collaborator: his brother Ira. Ira had never lost his boyhood interest in reading. In his early 20s, he published some humorous poetry and short funny articles. He also wrote some song lyrics for his own amusement. These efforts earned him almost nothing. He had to work at odd jobs to make enough money to live on.

"To the family Ira seemed a floating soul; he who had begun as the family scholar was now the drifter, haunting the movies and reading," note biographers Edward Jablonski and Edward D. Stewart. "'I read without plan or purpose. To tell the truth, I was at a complete loss, and I didn't care.'"[6]

His attitude soon changed. In 1918, he wrote a song with George called "The Real American Folk Song (Is a Rag)," which became part of a musical revue. That encouraged him to continue writing songs. He adopted the name of "Arthur Francis," combining the first names of his two youngest siblings, so that it wouldn't appear he was just trying to cash in on George's increasing fame. He collaborated with several composers over the next three years before joining George for good and using his own name again.

Arthur Gershwin—the youngest Gershwin—also enjoyed songwriting. Unfortunately, he wasn't very successful and became a stockbroker instead.

George and Ira may have had nothing in common as boys, but as young men their personalities meshed perfectly. Ira's lyrics worked well with George's music. From then on they would be virtually inseparable. The musical also made Fred and Adele Astaire into big stars, just as George had hoped when all three of them were jammed into his tiny cubicle at Remick's.

In 1925, George achieved a singular distinction when *Time* magazine put his picture on the cover. He was the first musician born in the United States to achieve this recognition. It marked a meteoric rise for a young man who just ten years earlier had been a high school dropout making fifteen dollars a week to plug songs. ◆

FBI's Top Cop

The year 1924 not only marked the debut of *Rhapsody in Blue*—one of the country's most famous musical compositions—but also an event that would eventually have wide-ranging effects on U.S. public policy. J. Edgar Hoover was appointed head of what was then known as the Bureau of Investigation (eleven years later it would become much better known as the Federal Bureau of Investigation, or FBI).

J. Edgar Hoover

Hoover was born in 1895 in Washington, D.C., to a family that had a long tradition of government service. He became a lawyer and in 1917 was hired by the Department of Justice. After World War I, he led a series of raids against suspected communists. While the methods he used were questionable, he acquired a reputation as someone who cared about his country. Soon afterward he was appointed head of the Bureau of Investigation. Several scandals had given the bureau a reputation for corruption. To restore public confidence, Hoover carefully recruited new agents and made sure that they had spotless reputations. He also established central registration for fingerprints and other innovations. Congress rewarded him by increasing the power and responsibilities of the bureau.

Starting in the mid-1930s, Hoover dramatically increased public awareness of the FBI by taking on many of the country's best-known gangsters in a series of highly publicized shootouts. His men were known as "Government Men." Shortened to *G-men*, the title helped give respect and popularity to the organization.

Hoover would remain FBI director for forty-eight years until his death in 1972, serving under eight presidents. During that time he became one of the most powerful men in the country. He also became increasingly controversial, because many people believed that he sometimes misused this power. He accumulated secret files on many people, including President John F. Kennedy and civil rights leader Martin Luther King, Jr.

George Gershwin (on the left) and his brother Ira pose for a formal portrait. The two of them were very different as boys but became virtually inseparable as young men and worked together very well.

Hard Times

"Swanee" had made Gershwin famous in the United States. *Rhapsody in Blue* extended that fame to Europe and the rest of the world. He was a star. As is the case with many stars, he became the guest of honor at many parties. Photographers frequently took his picture. It helped that he was very photogenic, and he wore expensive suits that made him look good.

It may have seemed to Gershwin that he could do no wrong. The success of his next musical, *Oh, Kay!,* provided additional proof. It contained one of his best-known songs, "Someone to Watch Over Me." But 1927's *Strike Up the Band* would interrupt his long string of successes. Most musicals followed a formula, using a famous star and a storyline that included romance, some problems to overcome, and a happy ending. *Strike Up the Band* was a satire about the folly of war. It had no superstars. As show business people say, it had no "legs" either. It quickly closed. Later that year, *Funny Face* flopped during out-of-town previews. Gershwin did some major rewriting and it became a hit—especially since Fred and Adele Astaire had the major roles.

In 1928, Gershwin made another trip to Europe. This time he went to Paris. He was accompanied by Ira, Ira's wife, Leonore, and their sister, Frankie. He wanted to write some new music. Even more important, he hoped that he could persuade a famous European composer to give him lessons. In spite of all his success, he believed that he needed a good teacher to help him write "serious" music. He had already studied for years with a man named Edward Kilenyi. He felt that working with a famous composer would help him even more.

At the height of his fame, he was constantly invited to parties, concerts, and other social gatherings. Often these gatherings included Gershwin playing his compositions on the piano. He enjoyed playing for other people and listening to their applause.

He wasn't successful in finding a teacher. Two noted composers, Maurice Ravel and Igor Stravinsky, both turned him down. So did Nadia Boulanger, a well-known teacher. They all said that his strength was his ability to improvise. They were afraid that formal lessons would destroy that spontaneity.

Gershwin became more successful in his composing. He wrote *An American in Paris*. As he described it, the aim was to show the way that an American tourist feels in Paris "as he strolls about the city, listens to various street noises, and absorbs the French atmosphere."[1] It even included the distinctive sound of taxi horns honking. When it debuted later that year, audiences loved it. It would become his second-most-famous composition after *Rhapsody in Blue*. It was later used as the basis of a popular movie starring Gene Kelly. But some critics said that it sounded as if an amateur had composed it.

Soon afterward, in 1929, the stock market crashed and the United States entered the Great Depression. At first it didn't seem to affect George. He wrote *Girl Crazy*, which made overnight stars of two previous unknown actresses, Ethel Merman and Ginger Rogers. Merman's rendition of George's song "I Got Rhythm" was the first of many triumphs during her long career on Broadway, while Rogers eventually became Fred Astaire's dancing partner in a number of hit movies in the 1930s and 1940s.

George and Ira Gershwin went to Hollywood to write the music for a new film called *Delicious*. They earned $100,000 for their work—a huge sum, especially with the nation still in the Depression. In 1931, the two men collaborated on the Broadway musical *Of Thee I Sing.* It was awarded the 1932 Pulitzer Prize for Drama. Because of the way Pulitzer Prizes were awarded at that time—there wasn't a category for composers—George couldn't share in the honors. Ira nearly declined the award, but George told him to accept it. Ira showed his unhappiness by hanging the certificate in his bathroom.

Despite these successes, George began to worry about his reputation. Even though he had written scores of popular songs and several successful musicals, he was afraid that he hadn't done anything truly great. For a while his mind was set at ease by the success of a huge open-air concert in New York. Nearly 18,000 people packed Lewisohn Stadium—an all-time record for the facility—for the first-ever all-Gershwin concert. Thousands more were turned away. Gershwin later described it as "the most exciting night I have ever had."[2]

The excitement soon wore off. Gershwin's next two works were failures. With the depression still raging, hardly anyone bought tickets for *Pardon My English.* With the Depression across the Atlantic, Adolf Hitler became German dictator in 1933. George's *Let 'Em Eat Cake* was a satire about a dictatorship similar to Hitler's coming to the United States. It didn't seem funny and quickly closed.

Despite these failures, Gershwin decided to raise his personal bar. In 1926, he had read a novel entitled *Porgy.* It was a love story that centered around two African Americans in the South. It was written by a white man named DuBose Heyward, who had spent much of his life working with African Americans and admired them. Heyward's wife, Dorothy, had made her husband's book into a successful play in 1927. The plot included many elements such as love and murder, laughter and revenge. Gershwin thought it would make an excellent opera and named it *Porgy and Bess* after the two principal characters. Because of the pressure of all his other work, he wasn't able to begin working on it until 1934. He and Ira traveled to Charleston, South Carolina, and spent several weeks working with Heyward. George finally completed the musical the following year. He was very happy with his work. The completed score was 700 pages long, and Gershwin believed that it was the finest thing he had ever done. It contains memorable songs such as "Summertime," "I Got Plenty O' Nuttin'," "Bess, You Is My Woman Now," "It Ain't Necessarily So," and "I Loves You, Porgy."

Even though Gershwin considered *Porgy and Bess* to be an opera, he decided to open it on Broadway. That may have been a mistake. The critics liked many of the songs, but felt that individual successes didn't make it an opera. On the other hand, it was far too serious to be successful as a Broadway musical. It closed before it could make a profit. George tried to put a good face on the situation, but there was no denying the evidence: *Porgy and Bess* was a flop.◆

The Coming of the New Deal

President Roosevelt

By the 1932 presidential election, the country had been in the grip of the Great Depression for three years. Millions of people were unemployed, and there didn't seem to be any end in sight. Many people blamed the policies of Republican president Herbert Hoover for the country's problems. Collections of primitive shacks that housed people who had lost their jobs and their homes were sarcastically called Hoovervilles.

The Democratic Party nominated Franklin Delano Roosevelt, the governor of New York, to run against Hoover. FDR, as he was familiarly known, told people on the campaign trail, "I pledge you, I pledge myself, to a new deal for the American people." The election wasn't close. Roosevelt won by a landslide.

As soon as he took office in 1933, Roosevelt encouraged people by saying, "The only thing we have to fear is fear itself." He made good on his campaign promises with what was known as the New Deal. The main difference between him and his predecessor was that he believed in using the power of the government to get the country out of the Depression. He began a number of programs, paid for by the government, to provide jobs for people. They included the Works Progress Administration (WPA), Civilian Conservation Corps (CCC), National Recovery Administration (NRA), and others. There were so many of these agencies that people often remarked that the government seemed like alphabet soup. The Social Security Administration, which provides government pensions for most workers when they retire, also came into existence at this time.

Many people were happy to see the government step in and take action. Others felt that Roosevelt's programs failed and made the Depression last longer than it would have otherwise. But there is no question that Roosevelt and his New Deal dramatically increased the amount of government involvement in national projects.

Regarded by most people as the greatest dancer in Hollywood history, Fred Astaire was born in 1899 and became a teenage friend of George Gershwin. He rose to film fame during the 1930s and 1940s, particularly with partner Ginger Rogers. He remained active in movies and television until a few years before his death in 1987.

Go West, Young Man

Gershwin was starting to worry. His last three shows had failed. Also, attendance at concerts of his music was falling off dramatically. One newspaper reported, "It was George Gershwin night at the Lewisohn Stadium and there were empty seats. That is news."[1] Gershwin was also beginning to complain of headaches.

He couldn't help noticing that many of his colleagues were heading west, to Southern California. Since movies had begun including synchronized sound in 1927—the so-called "talkies"—movie attendance had taken off. Hollywood studios were paying big money for writing just a few songs. There was a string attached. In return for all that money, the studios would have control of the songs.

The studio executives read the newspapers too. They noticed that Gershwin might be losing his touch. They were also afraid that his interest in opera meant that he wasn't interested in writing popular music anymore. Gershwin was able to convince them that he would write what they wanted. In the fall of 1936 he left for California with Ira and Leonore. They rented a large house with a tennis court in Beverly Hills. A neighbor was famous modern composer Arnold Schoenberg, who played a lot of tennis with George. Gershwin also wanted Schoenberg to become his teacher, though nothing ever came of that.

Gershwin had mixed feelings about his new life in Southern California. "Look at this place—desert," he told a friend. "Here they drill four holes and plant palm trees. Then they drill a bigger hole and install a swimming pool. Finally they build a still larger, deeper hole and put up a house. It's unbelievable."[2]

He was often unhappy with the working conditions. He told a friend, "I'm not the kind of composer where a man tells me I need five songs for this film, now compose. I can't do that anymore. I'm dying to get back to New York to compose when I want to."[3]

There was also a lot about California to like. Gershwin enjoyed taking long hikes in the warm sunshine. He spent many evenings with friends who had also moved across the country. Being in Hollywood gave him the opportunity to work again with Fred Astaire and Ginger Rogers, who by then had become regular partners. And as Gershwin explained to Frankie when she visited him, "I'm here to make enough money with movies so I don't have to think of money anymore. Because I want to work on American music: symphonies, chamber music, opera."[4]

Yet in spite of living with his brother and his brother's wife and enjoying frequent evenings with his friends, he felt lonely. He wanted to fall in love, but couldn't find a suitable partner. In addition, his headaches were getting worse. The pain was sometimes so intense that he would collapse. Hospital tests were inconclusive. One doctor offered to administer a spinal tap. It would be a very painful procedure, and Gershwin decided not to go through with it.

On July 9, Gershwin collapsed and went into a coma. He was rushed to a hospital. Since he was unconscious, doctors could finally perform a spinal tap. It revealed the existence of a large brain tumor. It was imperative to operate as quickly as possible if there was any hope of saving his life. In spite of a five-hour operation to remove the tumor, George Gershwin died on the morning of July 11, 1937. He was only thirty-eight.

People were shocked.

"He was so completely the personification of vitality and resonant health that a physical or mental breakdown seemed altogether unthinkable," wrote one man. "The care of his physical being was almost a mania with him."[5]

"His death seems to me the most tragic thing that I have ever known,"[6] wrote another.

It was especially hard on Ira. "After the funeral services in New York in July 1937 I returned to our house in Beverly Hills in a deep and unshakeable state of despondency," he wrote. "Days and nights passed in a blur. Then one afternoon I got to the record player and somehow found myself putting on the Fred Astaire–Johnny Green recordings of the *Shall We Dance* score—most of which had been written in that very room less than a year before. In a few moments the room was filled with gaiety and rhythm, and I felt that George, smiling and approving, was there listening with me—and grief vanished."[7]

While it would take several years for Ira to resume working, his songwriting career lasted another two decades. His greatest hit was "Long Ago and Far Away," which he wrote for composer Jerome Kern to use in the 1944 movie *Cover Girl.* Working with his wife Leonore, he spent much of the rest of his life promoting his brother's musical legacy. One of the highlights of this legacy came in 1976 when *Porgy and Bess* finally achieved the success that George envisioned for it, with a full-scale production by the Houston Opera. The world-famous Metropolitan Opera in New York City performed it for the first time in 1985. Many people now believe that *Porgy and Bess* is the best opera ever written by an American.

Rhapsody in Blue, Gershwin's most famous composition, has been used in many ways. In 1945, a film called *Rhapsody in Blue* was made about his life, although it wasn't very accurate. Film director Woody Allen used the music in his 1979 movie *Manhattan.* Russian ice skater Ilia Kulik's gold medal–winning performance in the 1998 Winter Olympics was accompanied by *Rhapsody in Blue.* The music was included in the Walt Disney movie *Fantasia 2000,* in which eight compositions are accompanied by animation. For many years, the song served as the theme for United Airlines in their television commercials.

Perhaps Gershwin's greatest honor came in 1998, the hundredth anniversary of his birth. He received an honorary Pulitzer Prize based on everything that he had written. The honor may also have been an effort to make up for when *Of Thee I Sing* won the Pulitzer Prize in 1932 but the award didn't include him.

As the famous American composer and conductor Leonard Bernstein wrote in the introduction to Charles Schwartz's book *Gershwin: His Life and Music,* "Gershwin was, and remains, one of the greatest voices that ever rang out in the history of American urban culture."[8]

Rodney Greenberg says, "The public has shown an enduring love for Gershwin. As with [Franz] Schubert, another born songwriter who died too young, we cannot help lamenting the loss of what might have been. But we can rejoice that, whatever trouble Mrs. Gershwin had with that son of hers, he grew up to enrich the music of our century."[9]

The Author of *Peter Pan*

J. M. Barrie

George Gershwin wasn't the only famous artistic figure to die in 1937. So did J. M. Barrie, the author of *Peter Pan*.

James Matthew Barrie was born in 1860 in the Scottish village of Kirriemuir. His father was a weaver and his mother raised the children. At the age of thirteen, James Matthew left home to go to school. He graduated from the University of Edinburgh in Scotland in 1882. He worked as a journalist for three years, then moved to London, England, in hopes of making a living as a freelance writer.

Barrie became successful with a combination of travel stories and novels before deciding to concentrate on writing plays. He was acquainted with many of the famous authors of the day, such as science fiction writer H. G. Wells and Arthur Conan Doyle, the creator of Sherlock Holmes.

Peter Pan had its premiere in 1904. The idea came from stories he made up for the five Davies boys, a family he befriended, as he had no children of his own. The title character is almost certainly named for Peter Davies. When the boys' parents died, Barrie became their unofficial guardian.

While he wrote more than forty plays and other works after *Peter Pan*, none came close to achieving its fame. Barrie became a baronet, an English nobleman, in 1913. In 1930 he was appointed chancellor of Edinburgh University; he died seven years later.

Peter Pan lives on. It has been made into movies several times. The most recent was *Peter Pan*, released in 2003, with a cast headed by Jeremy Sumpter, Jason Isaacs, Lynn Redgrave, Ludivine Sagnier, and Olivia Williams. Another notable version was 1991's *Hook*. Directed by Steven Spielberg, it starred Robin Williams, Dustin Hoffman, Julia Roberts, and Bob Hoskins.

In 2004, the movie *Finding Neverland* featured Johnny Depp, Kate Winslet, Dustin Hoffman, and Julie Christie. It is a mystical story based on Barrie's life.

Peter Pan is also still performed in the theater. In 1999, a production was staged in New York City's Gershwin Theater. A revival of that production, starring Olympic gymnast Cathy Rigby, toured the United States in 2004–2005 to honor the 100th anniversary of the show.

Chronology

1898	Born on September 26 in New York City
1913	Begins taking piano lessons with Charles Hambitzer
1914	Drops out of school and begins working on Tin Pan Alley for Jerome H. Remick and Company
1916	Publishes first song
1917	Quits at Remick's; gets job as rehearsal pianist
1918	"The Real American Folk Song (Is a Rag)," his first collaboration with Ira, premieres on Broadway
1919	Writes *La, La, Lucille,* his first complete Broadway score
1920	Publishes "Swanee," his first big hit
1923	Travels to Europe
1924	*Rhapsody in Blue* premieres
1928	Travels to Paris; *An American in Paris* premieres
1930	Goes to Hollywood to write score for *Delicious*
1932	First all-Gershwin concert sets attendance record at Lewisohn Stadium in New York
1934	Begins working on *Porgy and Bess*
1935	*Porgy and Bess* premieres
1936	Travels to Hollywood, California, with his brother Ira and Ira's wife, Leonore
1937	Dies of a brain tumor on July 11 in Hollywood
1959	*Porgy and Bess* is made into a movie
1983	The Uris, a Broadway theater, is renamed the Gershwin in honor of George and Ira
1998	Awarded a special Pulitzer Prize for his body of work

Timeline in History

1875	French composer Maurice Ravel is born.
1877	Thomas Edison invents the phonograph.
1882	Russian composer Igor Stravinsky is born.
1888	Composer Irving Berlin is born.
1896	Ira Gershwin is born.
1898	The United States defeats Spain in the Spanish-American War.
1903	Jack London publishes his novel *The Call of the Wild.*
1907	Impresario Florenz Ziegfeld stages the first *Ziegfeld's Follies* in New York City.
1911	Norwegian explorer Roald Amundsen becomes the first person to reach the South Pole.
1912	The ocean liner *Titanic* sinks on her maiden voyage after striking an iceberg.
1914	The Panama Canal opens.
1919	The Treaty of Versailles formally ends World War I and imposes harsh surrender terms on Germany.
1920	John T. Thompson, a retired U.S. Army officer, receives a patent for the submachine gun he designs; it becomes known as the tommy gun.
1924	The first Winter Olympic Games are held in Chamonix, France; they include 293 athletes from sixteen nations.
1927	*The Jazz Singer,* the first "talkie" (movie with synchronized sound), makes its debut.
1929	The stock market crash causes the Great Depression.
1932	Franklin Delano Roosevelt is elected to the first of his four terms as U.S. President.
1933	Adolf Hitler becomes German dictator and begins establishing concentration camps.
1937	Maurice Ravel dies.
1938	Irving Berlin writes "God Bless America."
1945	*Rhapsody in Blue,* a movie about Gershwin's life, is released.
1983	Ira Gershwin dies.
1989	Irving Berlin dies.
2000	*George Gershwin Alone,* a play about Gershwin's life that includes much of his music, premieres in West Hollywood, California, and moves to Broadway the following year.
2004	*De-Lovely*, a movie about songwriter Cole Porter starring Kevin Kline and Ashley Judd, premieres.

Glossary

arsenals (AR-seh-nuhls)—collections of military weapons.

audition (aw-DIH-shun)—a tryout for a musical or theatrical role.

blackface (BLACK-face)—makeup applied to a white actor who is playing the part of an African American.

bookmaker (BOOK-may-ker)—a person who determines gambling odds, then collects and pays off bets.

boycott (BOY-cot)—to show dissatisfaction by refusing to associate with or to buy from an individual or group.

cold war—a conflict of differences among nations that stops short of physical violence or military action.

concerto (con-CHAIR-toe)—a musical composition, usually in three movements, for orchestra and solo instrument.

crescendo (kreh-SHEN-doe)—an increase in the intensity of sound.

lyricist (LEER-uh-cyst)—a person who writes the words to a song.

opera (AH-p'rah)—a musical drama in which the actors sing the dialogue.

recluse (RECK-loose)—a person who keeps to himself or herself.

royalty (ROY-uhl-tee)—a payment to a composer or writer for each copy of a work sold.

vaudeville (VAWD-vil)—a stage entertainment consisting of several different types of acts.

Chapter 2
From the Streets to the Piano

1. Rodney Greenberg, *George Gershwin* (London: Phaidon Press Limited, 1998), p. 11.

2. Deena Rosenberg, *Fascinating Rhythm: The Collaboration of George and Ira Gershwin* (New York: Plume Penguin, 1993), p. 6.

3. Edward Jablonski, *Gershwin* (New York: Doubleday, 1987), p. 7.

4. Rosenberg, p. 10.

5. Ibid., p. 11.

6. Ibid., p. 12.

Chapter 3
Tin Pan Alley

1. Deena Rosenberg, *Fascinating Rhythm: The Collaboration of George and Ira Gershwin* (New York: Plume Penguin, 1993), p. 13.

2. Edward Jablonski, *Gershwin* (New York: Doubleday, 1987), p. 17.

Chapter 4
Rhapsody in Blue

1. Rodney Greenberg, *George Gershwin* (London: Phaidon Press Limited, 1998), p. 52.

2. Edward Jablonski, *Gershwin* (New York: Doubleday, 1987), p. 65.

3. Charles Schwartz, *Gershwin: His Life and Music.* New York: The Bobbs-Merrill Company, 1973), p. 77.

4. Ibid., p. 87.

5. Jablonski, p. 67.

6. Edward Jablonski and Lawrence D. Stewart, *The Gershwin Years: George and Ira* (New York: Da Capo Press, 1996), p. 58.

Chapter 5
Hard Times

1. Edward Jablonski, *Gershwin* (New York: Doubleday, 1987), p. 177.

2. Charles Schwartz, *Gershwin: His Life and Music.* New York: The Bobbs-Merrill Company, 1973), p. 226.

Chapter 6
Go West, Young Man

1. Rodney Greenberg, *George Gershwin* (London: Phaidon Press Limited, 1998), p. 200.

2. Ibid., p. 203.

3. Ibid., p. 208.

4. Ibid., p. 209.

5. Deena Rosenberg, *Fascinating Rhythm: The Collaboration of George and Ira Gershwin* (New York: Plume Penguin, 1993), p. 366.

6. Ibid., p. 368.

7. Ibid., p. 369.

8. Charles Schwartz, *Gershwin: His Life and Music.* New York: The Bobbs-Merrill Company, 1973), p. xii.

9. Greenberg, p. 220.

For Further Reading

For Young Adults

Gershwin, George. *The Music of George Gershwin*. Milwaukee: Hal Leonard Corporation, 1997.

Kresh, Paul. *American Rhapsody: The Story of George Gershwin*. New York: Dutton Books, 1988.

Reef, Catherine. *George Gershwin: American Composer*. Greensboro, N.C.: Morgan Reynolds, Inc., 2000.

Vernon, Roland. *Introducing Gershwin*. Broomall, Pa.: Chelsea House Publishers, 2001.

Whiting, Jim. *The Life and Times of Irving Berlin*. Masters of Music. Hockessin, Del.: Mitchell Lane Publishers, 2004.

Works Consulted

Greenberg, Rodney. *George Gershwin*. London: Phaidon Press Limited, 1998.

Jablonski, Edward. *Gershwin*. New York: Doubleday, 1987.

Jablonski, Edward, and Lawrence D. Stewart. *The Gershwin Years: George and Ira*. New York: Da Capo Press, 1996.

Rosenberg, Deena. *Fascinating Rhythm: The Collaboration of George and Ira Gershwin*. New York: Plume Penguin, 1993.

Schaap, Dick. *The 1984 Olympic Games*. New York: Random House, 1984.

Schwartz, Charles. *Gershwin: His Life and Music*. New York: The Bobbs-Merrill Company, 1973.

On the Internet

George and Ira Gershwin: The Official Web Site
http://www.gershwin.com
Classical Net: "George Gershwin"
http://www.classical.net/music/comp.lst/gershwin.html
Arts Alive! "George Gershwin"
www.artsalive.ca/en/mus/greatcomposers/gershwin.html
Sports and Politics
Stoneridge Water Polo, "Water Polo & Politics"
http://www.stoneridgewaterpolo.com/history/
Jewish Virtual Library, "The Nazi Olympics"
http://www.us-israel.org/jsource/Holocaust/olympics.html
The Spanish-American War
"The World of 1898: The Spanish-American War"
http://www.loc.gov/rr/hispanic/1898/intro.html

For Further Reading (Cont'd)

"Crucible of Empire: The Spanish-American War"
http://www.pbs.org/crucible/
"J. Edgar Hoover, 1895–1972"
http://www.pbs.org/wgbh/amex/eleanor/peopleevents/pande07.html
The Coming of the New Deal
"President Franklin Delano Roosevelt and the New Deal, 1933–1945"
http://memory.loc.gov/learn/features/timeline/depwwii/newdeal/newdeal.html
Franklin D. Roosevelt
http://www.whitehouse.gov/history/presidents/fr32.html
The Author of *Peter Pan*
Scottish Authors, "Sir J. M. Barrie"
http://www.slainte.org.uk/scotauth/barridsw.htm
Books and Writers, "J. M. Barrie"
http://www.kirjasto.sci.fi/jmbarrie.htm

Selected Works

Opera
Porgy and Bess

Orchestral Works
Rhapsody in Blue
An American in Paris
Cuban Overture
Piano Concerto in F

Musicals
La, La, Lucille
Lady, Be Good!
Oh, Kay!
Funny Face
Strike Up the Band
Girl Crazy

Of Thee I Sing
Let 'Em Eat Cake

Movie Scores
Shall We Dance?
A Damsel in Distress
The Goldwyn Follies

Songs
Swanee
I'll Build a Stairway to Paradise
Someone to Watch Over Me
I Got Rhythm
Summertime
Let's Call the Whole Thing Off
It Ain't Necessary

Index